teen suicide

Lorena Huddle
and Jay Schleifer

ROSEN
PUBLISHING®

New York

Published in 2012 by The Rosen Publishing Group, Inc.
29 East 21st Street, New York, NY 10010

First Edition

Library of Congress Cataloging-in-Publication Data

Huddle, Lorena.
Teen suicide / Lorena Huddle, Jay Schleifer.—1st ed.
   p. cm.—(Teen mental health)
Includes bibliographical references and index.
 ISBN 978-1-4488-4586-6 (library binding)
1. Teenagers—Suicidal behavior—United States—Juvenile litera-
ture. 2. Suicide—United States—Prevention—Juvenile literature. 3.
Teenagers—Mental health—United States—Juvenile literature. I.
Schleifer, Jay. II. Title. III. Series.
HV6546.H83 2012
362.280835'0973—dc22

                                                                    2011006337

Manufactured in the United States of America

CPSIA Compliance Information: Batch #S11YA: For further information, contact Rosen Publishing, New York, New York,
at 1-800-237-9932.

Teen Suicide

contents

chapter one

Why Do Teens Kill Themselves?

Today only accidents and homicide claim the lives of more young people than suicide. According to the Centers for Disease Control and Prevention (CDC), in 2007 nearly 4,140 people between the ages of fifteen and twenty-four were reported to have killed themselves. Suicide among the same age group accounts for about 12.2 percent of all deaths each year.

Teens today are confronting suicide much more often than their parents did when they were young. There were nearly three times as many teen suicides in 2007 as there

4

were in 1960. In 2009, as stated by the CDC, 13.8 percent of U.S. high school students claimed that they had seriously thought about committing suicide during the twelve months preceding the survey; 6.3 percent of the students reported that they had actually attempted suicide at least once during that same period.

It's not surprising that suicide rates have increased dramatically in the last fifty years. The teen years are

Tina Meier *(right)* congratulates Missouri governor Matt Blunt after he signed a bill to protect Missouri children from cyberbullying and cyberstalking. Meier's teen daughter, Megan, committed suicide after she received cruel messages on her MySpace page.

typically marked by feelings of insecurity and depression. Teens also have to deal with pressures from parents, peers, and society in general. Recently these pressures have become even more extreme. Illegal drug use is a much more common problem for teens today than for past generations. A 2009 Monitoring the Future study, compiled by the University of Michigan, found that most illegal drug use by high school students had decreased since 1999 (the exception was the use of marijuana). Many experts believe that there is no doubt that suicide and drug use are linked: The National Violent Death Reporting System announced in 2009 that for those tested for substance abuse at the time of death, sixteen states revealed that one-third of those who died by suicide tested positive for alcohol at the time of death, and almost one in five had evidence of opiates (including heroin and prescription pain killers).

In addition to the usual issues teens have faced in the past, more and more young people are troubled by problems that were once considered only adult concerns. Complicated issues of birth control, pregnancy, and sexually transmitted diseases (STDs) can create further problems for teens. In addition, teens who think they may be bisexual or gay often experience feelings of extreme isolation and depression. Many come to consider suicide the only solution. In 2010, several teen suicides resulted from bullying and cyberbullying incidents.

Many teens today are growing up in environments where violence and crime are common. Others may be living with abusive parents and feel unsafe in their own homes. It may be difficult for these teens to find a place where they can be safe or to find people whom they can trust.

Feelings of Hopelessness and Despair

Committing suicide used to be considered a disgraceful act. In parts of Europe, there was a time when people who killed themselves were buried at crossroads. This was intended to draw attention and shame to the suicide. Many religions also condemn suicide. Judaism, Christianity, and Islam consider it morally wrong.

Suicide was once considered a crime in the United States. As the reasons why people commit suicide have become better understood, antisuicide laws in many states have been removed. Today, suicide is not classified as a crime in any U.S. state. People have found that punishing someone who has attempted suicide only adds to his or her depression, which could lead to another suicide attempt.

Over time there have been more efforts to help people understand why someone would commit suicide. Sometimes when people hear about suicide they may think about copying suicide victims. There have been stories about suicides, both fictional and real, that may make suicide seem romantic or glamorous. For example, in 1594 William Shakespeare wrote the play *Romeo and Juliet*, in which the two title characters who were in love, when faced with the idea that they could not be together, committed suicide.

Another example is the 1994 suicide of Kurt Cobain, the lead singer of the rock band Nirvana. Cobain had many fans. When he killed himself, some young people thought that suicide might be cool. Cobain's wife, Courtney Love, has publicly told his fans that what her husband did was selfish and wrong. Cobain also left behind a daughter

Rock musician Kurt Cobain committed suicide at the age of twenty-seven. He became a cultural icon for many young people, but his widow, Courtney Love, said his suicide "just wasn't cool." Their daughter would never know her father.

who will never know her father.

Suicide is not romantic or cool. No matter how troubled a suicide victim may have been, his or her death never helps anyone. In most cases, a suicide attempt is really a cry for help. People who commit suicide often believe that their problems are too big and scary for them to ever solve. But no matter how big a problem may be, there is a better solution. Help is always available.

Why Do Teens Get So Depressed?

It is not possible to list all the reasons why teens decide to take their own lives. Some of the more common causes are listed in the following:

- Feeling rejected, abandoned, or alone
- Low self-esteem, or feeling like a failure

- Feeling ashamed and unworthy of forgiveness
- Pressures at school, home, or with friends
- Problems with alcohol or drugs
- Feelings of hopelessness or depression (sadness that does not go away and has no clear cause)
- Feeling afraid of something or someone

Frequently, teens who kill themselves have had upsetting experiences of some kind. Young suicide victims may explain their feelings in notes that they leave behind.

Some of their reasons may include the following:

- Breaking up with a boyfriend or girlfriend
- Doing poorly in school or not being accepted for a job or by a college
- Not doing well in sports or other activities
- Being worried about letting down family members or friends
- Being gay and feeling guilty or afraid of not being accepted
- Moving and leaving friends behind or having a good friend move away
- Divorce or other problems in the family (such as alcohol, drugs, or sexual abuse)
- Being unable to repay a large debt
- A serious physical injury or illness
- Being responsible for an injury to another person
- Having committed a serious crime
- The death of a parent, close friend, or other family member

Suicidal behavior does not necessarily happen all at once. The breakup of a two-parent family, whether from divorce, desertion, or the death of a parent, makes young people more vulnerable to suicidal behavior.

Some of the problems that teen suicide victims list may seem much more serious than others. All of these problems are very real to the people who experience them.

These problems can also trigger some uncomfortable feelings. For example, parents divorcing may make a teen feel rejected and abandoned. He or she may not be able to cope with new pressures at home.

The teen years are full of powerful and confusing emotions that can last a long time. Young people who say they want to die often think these painful feelings will never go away. They are wrong. Working through these feelings may take a lot of time and effort. However, it is possible to get help and turn your life around.

The actual number of teenagers who commit suicide may be higher than the reported figures. The reason for this is because it can be difficult to determine whether a death was an accident or on purpose. If someone commits suicide without leaving a note, the death may be categorized as an accident.

There are other suicides that the authorities don't know about, because people close to the victim often try to hide it. Many families of suicide victims will try to make the suicide look like an accident. They are ashamed that their child took his or her own life. They believe it says something bad about them.

But people need to know and face the truth about suicide. Maybe then it will be easier to stop suicide and suicide attempts.

Some Misconceptions About Suicide

When you hear or see the word "misconception" it usually means a misunderstanding or misbelief. The term "myth" is also used to refer to a mistaken belief or idea. Some misconceptions can be dangerous, because they may encourage people to take harmful actions. The following are a few misunderstandings about teen suicide:

- **Teens who talk about killing themselves never really do.** The majority of suicide victims told someone that they were planning to take their own lives. If someone you know says he or she is considering suicide, you should take it seriously. This person needs immediate help. Suicide isn't an appropriate method to solve problems. If someone is talking about suicide to get attention, that person's problem-solving skills have been impaired. You should encourage him or her to talk to a trusted adult, such as a teacher, school counselor, minister, or rabbi, for advice.

- **Teens usually commit suicide without any warning.** This misconception is related to the first one. Usually, young people who are thinking about suicide let someone know in the weeks prior to their death. If they don't say so directly, they might give out certain hints. For example, a teenager who is thinking about suicide might start giving away important personal belongings. There are almost always warning signs.

12

- **Talking about suicide might trigger someone to actually attempt it.** If you think someone is considering suicide, you should always talk to that person about it. You won't be putting ideas into his or her head. Young people need to talk about their unhappiness—discussing suicidal thoughts openly and showing that you care is one of the most helpful things a person can do. Your concern may give them strength to overcome their problems or to seek professional help.

Talking to a depressed person who is thinking about suicide can be tricky. Comfort your friend and show you care, but before offering specific advice, it is always better to talk with an expert or a trusted adult.

Working Through Your Problems

If you feel that suicide is the only way to end your problems, try talking to someone. Find an older sibling, a friend, a teacher, a religious leader or any trusted adult. They can help you to see that there are always other answers and choices in resolving your problems. If there isn't someone around to talk to, or you prefer to talk anonymously, call directory assistance and ask the operator for a local suicide hotline number. Suicide hotlines can also be found listed in your local telephone book. The national suicide hotline in the United States is (800) 784-2433 (800-SUICIDE; the Web address is http://suicidehotlines.com). Sometimes when you can talk about your problem with another person, it may not seem as bad as it did before.

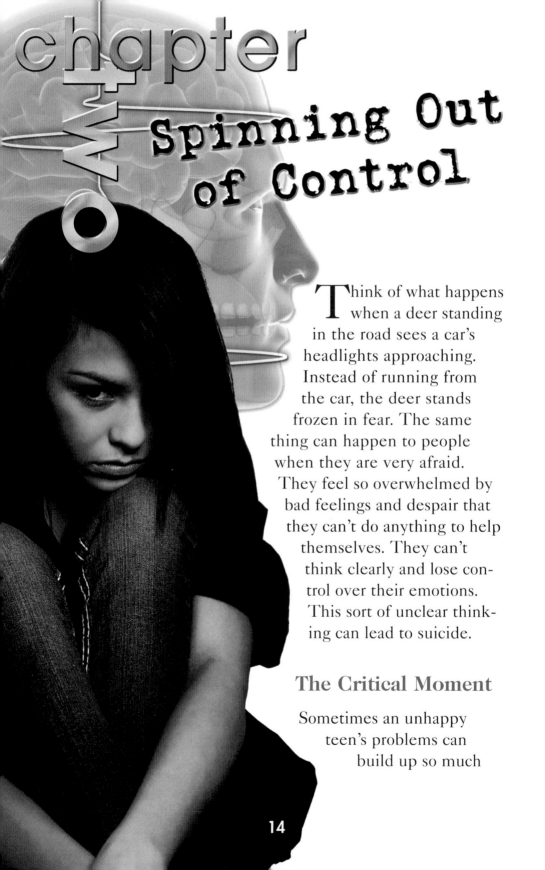

chapter TWO

Spinning Out of Control

Think of what happens when a deer standing in the road sees a car's headlights approaching. Instead of running from the car, the deer stands frozen in fear. The same thing can happen to people when they are very afraid. They feel so overwhelmed by bad feelings and despair that they can't do anything to help themselves. They can't think clearly and lose control over their emotions. This sort of unclear thinking can lead to suicide.

The Critical Moment

Sometimes an unhappy teen's problems can build up so much

that they lead to a personal crisis. This moment is called the breaking point. A person may feel so overwhelmed that he or she stops thinking clearly.

The problem may begin at home. An alcoholic parent, for example, may be out of work and difficult to live with. Family problems may lead to other problems at school. With added stress the teen may turn to drugs or alcohol as an escape. As the problems get more serious, he or she may be headed for a crisis. The teen could then begin to lose control over his or her emotions and turn to suicide.

Young people face pressures every day. Fortunately, most teens are able to handle crisis situations. Teens with good self-esteem believe in their own ability to solve problems. They also know they can find help if they need it. They take control of their own lives.

Not all young people have such a healthy self-image. They may lack courage and confidence

Depression is a major risk factor of suicide. Teens who have low self-esteem or who set high standards for themselves and don't achieve them can have feelings of disappointment and helplessness.

at a time of a crisis. They may feel helpless and unable to control the feelings that caused their crisis.

Feeling helpless in a crisis can make some young people think about suicide. They begin to see suicide as a way out of their problems. Once they make the decision to commit suicide, they usually become calm. They no longer feel helpless, because they have decided to take action. Others may mistakenly think that these young people are getting better and decide that they no longer need help. But this is the time when they will need help the most. If no one steps in to help, suicidal teenagers will try to end their lives.

The truth is that things could get better for troubled teens. But teenagers who think they want to die cannot see this on their own. When they reach a crisis, they need someone to reach out and show them a better way.

Feeling Down and Hopeless

Although most people are eventually able to lift themselves from their sadness, there are others who have a much harder time. They find that they are easily trapped by their feelings. They may feel unable to see past their problems and hopelessness.

Many people who find that they cannot overcome their negative feelings may be suffering from an illness called depression. For them, depression may seem endless and uncontrollable. The reasons why some people suffer from depression are not clear. It could be a combination of their experiences and the levels of certain chemicals in their brains.

There are millions of people who cope with this illness at some point in their lives. About one out of every five teenagers suffers from depression, according to the media company IRIS Ed Online. The symptoms can affect not only a person's emotions but also his or her physical health.

Because problems can seem much worse to a depressed person than to others, he or she will reach a crisis much more easily. People who suffer from depressive illnesses are the group most at risk for committing suicide. According to the National Institute of Mental Health, more than 90 percent of people who die by suicide have one or more of the following risk factors: depression or other mental disorder, substance abuse (alcohol or drugs), or conduct disorder (running away, criminal activity, or antisocial behavior).

But depression does not have to lead to suicide. There are ways to treat depression, with both medication

These positron emission tomography (PET) scans show a normal brain scan (top) and one that exhibits depression (bottom). Depression has physical, emotional, and mental symptoms; however, it is treatable.

and therapy. If you think that you may be suffering from depression, a doctor or counselor can tell you how to get help.

Copycat or Cluster Suicides

In recent years there have been a number of cluster suicides. In cluster suicides (also called copycat suicides) one

These parents almost lost their fifteen-year-old daughter from a suicide attempt a day after her friend committed suicide. Their daughter and six other teens tried to copy their friend's suicide and used a social networking site to plan their actions.

or more troubled teens imitate another person who has committed suicide. They "copy" that person by killing themselves in a similar way. The CDC announced in 2009 that suicide clusters accounted for one hundred to two hundred deaths every year. The CDC defines a suicide cluster as "a group of suicides or suicide attempts, or both, that occur closer together in time and space than would normally be expected in a given community."

Everyone is very sad when a young person takes his or her own life. But the sadness doesn't always end there. Soon afterward other students at the same school might take their lives in the same way.

Cluster suicides have happened in many towns across the country. The news media report a death in one state. Suddenly there are deaths like it thousands of miles away.

An Attempt to Get Help

Some teens see suicide as a way to get attention. They see it as a way to be famous. But they don't understand that they won't be around to enjoy the attention or the fame. Maybe you have felt depressed enough to think about suicide. Perhaps the idea of trying to get attention that way may not make sense to you. Feelings of depression can keep a person from thinking clearly. It can make someone feel confused.

Troubled teens are more likely to get the help they need when the people who care for them can tell that a suicide may be coming.

MYTHS AND FACTS

Myth: Most teens who are extremely depressed do not actually think about killing themselves.

Fact: Most teens who are very depressed do think about suicide. Between 15 percent and 30 percent of those teens who think about it attempt it, according to IRIS Ed Online. Nearly two thousand teens kill themselves annually, making suicide the third leading cause of death among teenagers.

Myth: Most suicides occur during the Christmas holiday in December.

Fact: The CDC's National Center for Health Statistics reported in 2009 that the suicide rate is, in fact, the lowest in the month of December. The suicide rate actually peaks in the spring and the fall.

Myth: If someone really wants to commit suicide, no one can talk that person out of it.

Fact: When a person is very depressed, that person has mixed feelings about dying. Usually the urge to end his or her life does not last forever. Most people who want to commit suicide do not want to end their lives, but instead want to stop the pain or despair that they are feeling. People who are extremely depressed may have a chemical imbalance in their brain. Depression can be effectively treated in 90 percent of cases with a combination of medication and therapy. People who are depressed need someone to show them that they care and understand.

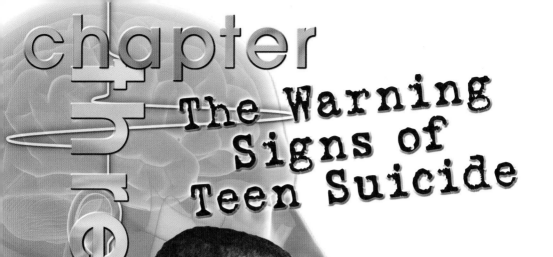

chapter three

The Warning Signs of Teen Suicide

Almost all people who consider suicide do not really want to end their lives. They may want to live but not under the prevailing circumstances. They want to be helped and will send out signs to let others know. When these signs are recognized, action can be taken to prevent teenage suicide. The more young people learn about the warning signs, the better their chances of preventing a friend's or loved one's suicide.

Some Indications of Suicide

Sometimes, teens send very clear indications, or signals, that they want to die. Here are some signs to watch for:

- **Trying to commit suicide.** The most obvious warning that a teen is suicidal is when the teen actually tries to take his or her life. Even if the attempt at suicide fails, it is an important sign. Just because someone has tried once and failed does not mean he or she won't try again. Anyone at this crisis point is at great risk. Getting professional help immediately is the only hope for making a lasting recovery.

- **Making threats or talking about suicide.** If you know someone who is threatening to commit suicide, you should take him or her seriously. Most people who try to kill themselves tell someone that they are thinking about it. Be a friend. Listen first, and then get help.

- **Talking about death.** Often, young people who are thinking about suicide will talk a lot about death. They may not talk about their own death—just the idea of dying. They may seem suddenly interested in methods of dying and the pain associated with each method.

- **Giving away favorite things.** Teens who are thinking about killing themselves will sometimes give away their personal belongings. For example, a teen who loves music might give his friend his prized portable media player.

These teens crashed their car. A possible sign of suicidal behavior is when a teen takes unnecessary risks, such as drinking alcohol or abusing drugs and then trying to drive a car or motorcycle.

Another young person might give away a favorite outfit or piece of jewelry or some other treasured possession.

- **Taking unnecessary risks.** Another way young people reveal that they are thinking about suicide is by taking unnecessary risks. Someone who never drinks alcohol or uses drugs might suddenly start abusing these substances. By taking dangerous risks, these teens are saying that they do not want to live.

Any behavior or conversations that are not normal could be a clue to a friend's true feelings. Pay attention to what you see and hear. It could save the life of someone you love.

- **Possible triggers: problems that pile up.** All teenagers go through rough times. Most get through these times without ever thinking about suicide. Some young people, however, may start to think about suicide when they reach a crisis point. If problems have piled up without relief, a teen may be headed for trouble. There is a limit to what a person can handle alone. When you (or a friend) feel overwhelmed, remember that help is always available. All you need to do is ask for it.

A suicidal teen might suffer severe depression for a long time. Signs of depression can include losing interest in friends and cutting classes.

The Emotional Signs of Depression

It is normal to feel sad. Most people realize that it won't last forever. Suicidal teens, on the other hand, are often

24

seriously depressed for a long time. They don't understand that their depression won't last forever. Most think it will never go away, and that death is the only way out.

Depressed teens often withdraw from their family and friends. They may seem very moody—happy and up one minute, sad and low the next. They may always seem bored and without energy. They might lose interest in the things they used to enjoy.

Depression, like suicide, has many of its own outward signs. The following are some warning signs of depression:

- No longer taking good care of himself or herself (wearing clothes that are not clean; not bathing or not keeping hair clean and combed; no longer caring what his or her room looks like).
- Not eating regularly and losing weight; or eating all the time and gaining weight rapidly.
- Drinking alcohol; abusing drugs.
- Fighting with parents, siblings, even friends and teachers; not being able to control anger or other strong feelings.
- Neglecting schoolwork; failing to attend classes.
- Spending less time with friends and family and more time alone.
- Becoming undependable on a job; calling in sick day after day.

Suicide does not happen suddenly. It is the result of negative feelings that build up over time. Identifying the warning signs can allow you to get help for someone before it is too late.

10 Great Questions to Ask a School Counselor

1. Why is suicide so common among teens?

2. Are there some teens who are more at risk of killing themselves?

3. If I suspect that a friend is considering suicide, what should I do?

4. What are the most common ways of committing suicide?

5. Why do males commit suicide more frequently than females do?

6. Are gay and lesbian teens at risk for suicide?

7. Can the risk of killing oneself be inherited?

8. Do alcohol and drug abuse increase the likelihood that someone will commit suicide?

9. Can a person predict suicide?

10. What if my friend refuses to talk with an adult about his suicidal thoughts and says that if I tell anyone he will surely kill himself?

chapter four

Prevention and Intervention

Suicide hotlines are telephone numbers that people can call to talk to a counselor about their feelings. It doesn't cost anything to call, and most hotlines can be reached at any time. Whenever a person is feeling alone or depressed, a crisis counselor will be available to talk about whatever is troubling that individual. Crisis centers are places where teens can

Call and crisis centers help people who are feeling emotionally stressed about their lives. The professionals who work in these centers connect teens who have suicidal thoughts with counselors who are trained to talk to them.

go to speak with counselors about their problems. Counselors are trained to help them release all of the feelings they may be keeping inside. They use a method called crisis intervention, or CI. CI helps people deal with those strong feelings that can cloud clear thinking. CI has four steps that help people want to stay alive. The steps are as follows:

> 1. **Getting the feelings out in the open.** Strong feelings are like steam in a kettle without a vent.

The pressure builds up until the steam is ready to explode out of the kettle.

Crisis counselors understand these feelings. They know that feelings of anger, frustration, and loneliness shouldn't be bottled up inside you. Instead, they need to be released before you can think clearly about a problem. But first you need to know that it's all right to have these feelings before you can let them out.

Counselors let you know these feelings are normal. Everyone has them. Counselors are trained to understand these feelings. They want to show teens that someone knows what it's like to feel so angry and alone that you want to die.

Being understood right away is often like a breath of air to a drowning person. Being able to release all of the emotions trapped inside can help you to view your problems more clearly. Then, you can begin to recover from feelings of anxiety or sadness.

2. **Discussing the problem.** Once your feelings are out in the open, it is easier to talk about your problem. The counselor will then ask more about the situation. You may be a victim of child abuse or be pregnant. Perhaps you are being bullied at school. The counselor will not try to solve your problem. A problem may be too complicated to solve over the phone. Most problems are not easily solved at once. It usually takes some more time. The counselor is there to help you bring out all the facts. By recognizing these

facts, you will have a clearer understanding of your problem. Then you can begin thinking about what part of the problem you want to work on solving first.

3. **Taking one step at a time, one day at a time.** Trying to solve a big problem is usually much easier when you try to solve one small part of it at a time. In the same way, a counselor will help you look at all the parts of your problem. He or she will begin with the part that is easiest to solve.

In fights with a parent, a teen could request an outside person to talk to both sides to help solve a monumental problem. The important thing to keep in mind is that there are several ways to solve most problems.

4. Solving problems in new ways. The final step in crisis intervention is to help the person see that most problems can be solved in several ways. In the case of fights with parents, for instance, a teen could ask an outside person to talk with both sides. The teen could move in with friends for a while. Another choice for the teen might be to do what the parents want but be allowed to ask something from them in return.

The important thing is for the teen to realize that there are other answers. When the teen knows that, he or she no longer feels trapped. He or she will probably no longer see death as the only way out.

With the help of the counselor and CI, you can begin to believe that there are other ways to solve problems. There are people who can help you cope with the challenges of life.

CI is only one of the many options that can help troubled teens. Trained people are ready to help in schools, in youth clubs and neighborhood groups, in hospitals, and even in police emergency units.

Someone who is trained to handle these particular problems should be involved in CI and crisis counseling. Dealing with a suicidal person is a delicate matter, because his or her feelings are so unstable. If someone you know is in danger of committing suicide, it is better to let a trained counselor handle the problem.

chapter five

What You Can Do to Help

What would you do if your best friend said that he or she wanted to commit suicide? What should you do or not do? The following are some guidelines that you might find helpful:

1. **Tell an adult immediately.** Whether or not it seems as though a friend is serious about committing suicide does not matter. If the friend says she or he wants to do it, there is a definite risk that the friend could actually kill herself or

himself. There is really no "right thing" you can say that will stop your friend from committing suicide. It is best to leave the situation to an adult who is trained in preventing suicide.

You can call the U.S. National Suicide Hotline [(800) SUICIDE] or National Suicide Prevention Lifeline Hotline [(800) 273-TALK]. School guidance counselors, doctors, or even the police can also be helpful. If you have friends and family that you trust, try talking to them as well. But it is best to find a person who is trained in handling suicidal feelings. (If you believe that your friend is in immediate danger, call 911.)

Talk to a school guidance counselor or another trusted adult if your friend says she wants to commit suicide. Even if your friend says that if you tell anyone, she will kill herself for sure, you need to speak with someone who is trained in suicide prevention.

2. **Do not attempt to deal with the dilemma yourself.** Trying to talk your friend out of suicide may make things worse, because you may say the

33

wrong thing. It is difficult to know what you should say to a person who is considering suicide. It is better to help him or her contact experts, like counselors or the police. It is normal to want to help a friend. However, trying to solve the problem yourself may do more harm than good.

3. **Take away all weapons or drugs.** Some people mistakenly believe that by removing the methods of suicide, such as pills or razors, they are stopping the person from committing suicide. Removing the means by which a person can commit suicide is only one step. The next step is to talk to an expert to find out how to help your friend.

4. **Do not keep it a secret.** Good friends are supposed to keep each other's secrets, but not if the secret is suicide! Tell an adult. Your friend might be upset at you for telling. But after he or she has been helped, your friend will thank you for it.

5. **Try to be a good friend.** Be understanding and supportive, even if your friend is angry with you for telling an adult about his or her suicidal feelings. Try to stay in touch. Keep calling and visiting. People with problems need to know that others care.

When a person is feeling depressed, they might not be much fun to be around. But this is a time when your friend needs you the most. By knowing what to do, you can help your friend cope with his or her problems.

chapter
six

Coping with Loss and Grief After Suicide

Even with all of the resources available, suicides still occur. Every one hundred minutes someone between the ages of fifteen and twenty-four commits suicide, according to Suicide.org.

For that person who completes suicide the problems are over. But for loved ones left behind, the problems are only beginning.

Anyone who has lost a loved one to suicide knows that

this is one of the worst kinds of grief. It can be even more painful and difficult to handle than the loss of a friend to illness or an accident.

Here are some of the feelings families and friends suffer when a young person takes his or her own life.

Distress and Disbelief

At first most family members and friends can't accept that a loved one killed himself or herself. They refuse to believe it. Maybe they knew about the victim's problems. Perhaps they had heard threats of suicide, but they cannot accept that it really has happened.

The shock one feels after the loss of a loved one can be overwhelming. It is hard to think of other things and get on with one's life. This pain can make simple things like sleeping and eating difficult. This is a time when friends and family need help to heal.

Sorrow

Death always brings sadness, no matter how it occurs. For years a loved one has been there with you. You are used to the sound of a voice. You know the face. You know the touch of a hand. Now that person is gone forever.

No one can face that kind of loss without reacting to it. For a long time you might wish for the loved one to come back, even though you know that it can never happen. People react in different ways to such feelings. Some cry. Others don't allow themselves to cry. Some people want to talk about the loved one and the way he or she

36

College students and friends hold a candlelight vigil at Rutgers University in New Brunswick, New Jersey, for Tyler Clementi, a student who killed himself two weeks earlier, after harassment over his sexuality.

died. Others can't bear to talk about it. All people feel pain, though. Sometimes it seems like the pain will never end. It may seem to go away, but it returns suddenly upon seeing a picture or hearing a special song. With time, though, people learn to live with the loss.

Dread and Disgrace

Sometimes a suicide brings feelings of fear and dread. Many people used to believe that suicide was a mental sickness handed down from parent to child. They feared that if one person in a family killed himself or herself, others in the family would do so, too.

If someone in your family commits suicide, this can certainly lead to feelings of depression and helplessness. But this does not mean you will want to take your own life, too. Suicide is not a trait passed down from one generation to the next. Suicide is always a choice. It happens when people decide to act on feelings of hopelessness and despair. Young people who have depression are more likely to have a family history of depression. In a 2009 CNN report, Dr. David Brent, a psychiatrist at the University of Pittsburgh Medical Center in Pennsylvania, said that a first-degree relative (a parent, brother or sister, or child) of a person who has committed suicide is four to six times more likely to attempt or complete a suicide. The National Institute of Mental Health gave two risk factors as family history of suicide and family history of mental disorder. Researchers have found that depression runs in families.

It is difficult to prove or disprove the notion that relatives of people who killed themselves imitate suicide. Experts believe that there is more evidence of copycat suicides among people who do not know suicide victims well but had heard about the event on the news. A person who is depressed always has other options. These feelings can be resolved safely.

A suicide can also bring about feelings of disgrace. Family members and friends may feel ashamed that they did not know about the person's problems. If they did know about the problems, they may feel ashamed because they did not do enough to help the suicide victim. Family members may also be ashamed because they may believe that other people will see the suicide as a sign that something was wrong with the family.

Resentment and Anger

Those left behind often feel resentful at the person who has committed suicide. "How could you do this to us?" they may ask. "Why did you choose to die instead of coming to us for help?" That anger often spills out into other parts of life. For instance, a child whose older brother or sister has committed suicide may suddenly begin to misbehave in school or have trouble with his or her schoolwork.

Blame and Guilt

Families and friends often blame themselves for the suicide of a loved one. They go over and over the last words and the last looks from the person. They try to think of anything they may have done to push the victim to suicide.

Dealing with Emotions After a Suicide

It is important for the families and friends of suicide victims to seek out professional help in their healing process. Counselors or other professionals can help by encouraging the family to talk about and explore their feelings. Families that do not seek help and bottle up their feelings may take a longer time to heal. Some may never heal at all. Ignoring how to cope with these feelings can be dangerous, because

This family is working with a counselor to help them heal after the suicide of a loved one. Counseling and therapy can help family members to talk about their pain and loss and work through feelings of anger and blame.

sometimes family members may become so depressed about the suicide that the family may begin to have other problems.

Counseling is also important in schools after the suicide of a student. Some schools have started suicide prevention programs. These may involve bringing in counselors to educate students and teachers about suicide, encouraging them to voice their feelings and talk to others about their problems. These counselors will also try to help students cope with the death of a suicide victim.

Schools may also set up peer counseling groups. These allow students to talk to each other about their feelings. Sometimes teens have an easier time expressing their feelings to others their age rather than to adults.

It is important that all people touched by a suicide have the chance to confront their emotions. Suicide can cause a crisis for anyone close to the victim. These feelings might lead to other suicides. Counseling with psychologists or with peer groups can stop copycat suicides before they begin.

Remember the lessons you have already learned from this book. If you have problems or feelings that you can't cope with, get help from someone you trust. Tell him or her how you feel. Furthermore, if a friend shares these kinds of problems or feelings with you, tell someone who can help you both.

Although most teens never think sincerely about killing themselves, the problem of suicide is very real and serious. No matter what the number of teen suicides may be, the number of lives affected is much greater. Many people are working to spread awareness about suicide and its prevention. By learning what can be done to help yourself or someone you know who is depressed, you can help stop the growing number of suicides.

bisexual Having sexual attraction to both males and females.

child abuse Deliberate harm of a child by an adult.

cluster suicide Two or more teen suicides that happen around the same time or in the same way; also called copycat suicide.

confront To come face-to-face with; encounter.

crisis When problems build up to a breaking point.

crisis center A call center or place where trained counselors help people who are having problems.

crisis intervention A way to help solve an immediate problem.

depression Overcome by feelings of sadness.

gay Having a sexual attraction to persons of the same sex.

guilt Blaming yourself; belief that you are at fault.

hotline A telephone line at a call center that is answered by professionals who are trained to help with a problem.

lesbian A woman who has romantic or sexual relationships only with other women.

misconception A misunderstanding or myth; a false or mistaken view.

opiates Drugs with morphinelike effects, derived from opium.

prevention A hindrance or obstacle.

psychiatrist A doctor who specializes in the prevention, diagnosis, and treatment of mental, addictive, and emotional disorders.

psychologist A person trained and educated to perform psychological (relating to the human mind and behavior) research, testing, and therapy (counseling).

resentment Anger, bitterness, or ill will.

shame Feeling as if you have done something wrong.

American Association of Suicidology
4201 Connecticut Avenue NW, Suite 408
Washington, DC 20008
(202) 237-2280
Web site: http://www.suicidology.org
This national association seeks to educate and train suicide prevention professionals to end the occurrence of suicide.

American Foundation for Suicide Prevention (AFSP)
120 Wall Street, Twenty-second Floor
New York, NY 10005
(888) 333-2377
Web site: http://www.afsp.org
A national nonprofit group, the AFSP provides research and outreach for people who may be at risk for suicide.

Centers for Disease Control and Prevention (CDC)
1600 Clifton Road
Atlanta, GA 30333
(800) 232-4636
Web site: http://www.cdc.gov
The CDC is the government organization that tries to protect human health by helping to prevent disease and injury.

Health Canada
Address Locator 0900C2
Ottawa, ON K1A 0K9
Canada
(866) 225-0709 or (613) 957-2991

Web site: http://www.hc-sc.gc.ca
Canada's federal health department's Web site provides
information on general health and promotes healthy
lifestyles for all Canadians.

The Jason Foundation, Inc.
18 Volunteer Drive
Hendersonville, TN 37075
(615) 264-2323
Web site: http://www.jasonfoundation.com
This organization works to prevent the silent epidemic of
youth suicide through its educational programs.

National Institute of Mental Health (NIMH)
U.S. Department of Health and Human Services
6001 Executive Boulevard, Room 8184, MSC 9663
Bethesda, MD 20892-9663
Web site: http://www.nimh.nih.gov
The NIMH is dedicated to the understanding and treat-
ment of mental illnesses.

National Suicide Hotline
(800) SUICIDE (784-2433)
The National Suicide Hotline is staffed around the clock,
24/7. The Web site, http://suicidehotlines.com, lists
hotlines in all fifty U.S. states and the District of
Columbia. It also provides crises lines for Canada
and for other countries around the world.

National Suicide Prevention Lifeline
(800) 273-TALK (8255)

This twenty-four-hour, seven-days-a-week hotline, which is
staffed by trained professionals, is dedicated to helping
those in crisis who are contemplating suicide.

Public Health Agency of Canada
1015 Arlington Street
Winnipeg, MB R3E 3R2
Canada
(204) 789-2000
Web site: http://www.phac-aspc.gc.ca
This agency helps promote the health of Canada's residents.

Suicide Awareness Voices of Education (SAVE)
9001 East Bloomington Freeway, Suite 150
Bloomington, MN 55420
(952) 946-7998
Web site: http://www.save.org
SAVE is a nonprofit organization mostly composed of sur-
vivors of suicide.

Web Sites

Due to the changing nature of Internet links, Rosen
Publishing has developed an online list of Web sites related
to the subject of this book. This site is updated regularly.
Please use this link to access the list:

http://www.rosenlinks.com/tmh/sui

Barnes, Donna Holland. *The Truth About Suicide*. New York, NY: Facts On File, 2010.

Cobain, Bev. *When Nothing Matters Anymore: A Survival Guide for Depressed Teens*. Rev. ed. Minneapolis, MN: Free Spirit Publishing, 2007.

Denkmire, Heather, and John V. Perritano. *The Truth About Anxiety and Depression*. 2nd ed. New York, NY: Facts On File, 2010.

Ford, Michael Thomas. *Suicide Notes: A Novel*. New York, NY: HarperTeen, 2008.

Giddens, Sandra. *Frequently Asked Questions About Suicide* (FAQ: Teen Life). New York, NY: Rosen Publishing, 2008.

Linderman, Mike, and Gary Brozek. *The Teen Whisperer: How to Break Through the Silence and Secrecy of Teenage Life*. Reprint ed. New York, NY: Harper Paperbacks, 2008.

Nelson, Richard E., and Judith C. Galas. *The Power to Prevent Suicide: A Guide for Teens Helping Teens*. Minneapolis, MN: Free Spirit Publishing, 2006.

Oliver, Lauren. *Before I Fall*. New York, NY: Harper, 2010.

Salomon, Ron. *Suicide* (Psychological Disorders). New York, NY: Chelsea House Publishers, 2007.

Schusterbauer, Emily. *Teen Suicide* (At Issue). Farmington Hills, MI: Greenhaven, 2009.

Simmons, Danette. *Teen Reflections: My Life, My Journey, My Story*. CreateSpace, 2010.

Williams, Heidi. *Teen Suicide* (Issues That Concern You). Farmington Hills, MI: Greenhaven, 2009.

Wohlenhaus, Kim. *Suicide Information for Teens: Health Tips About Suicide Causes and Prevention* (Teen Health). 2nd ed. Detroit, MI: Omnigraphics, 2010.

About the Authors

Lorena Huddle, a writer, has four children and lives in Clinton County, Michigan.

Jay Schleifer is an editor and writer who grew up in New York City. He has written numerous books for young people and now resides in Florida.

Photo Credits